SWIFT WALKER

A Journey Around The Oceans

Written by VERLYN TARLTON

Illustrated by NORMA ANDRIANI EKA PUTRI

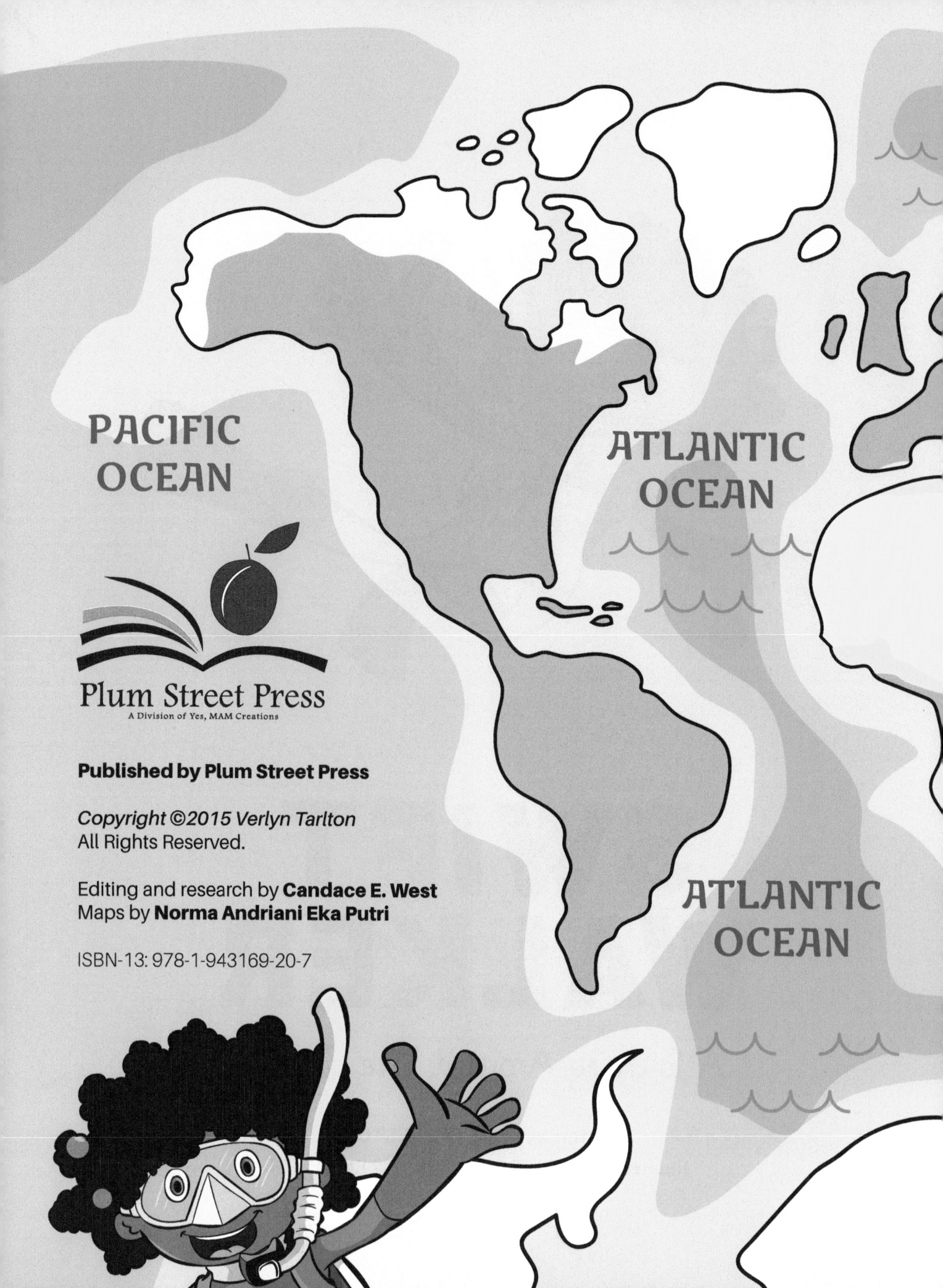

PACIFIC
OCEAN

ATLANTIC
OCEAN

ATLANTIC
OCEAN

Plum Street Press
A Division of Yes, MAM Creations

Published by Plum Street Press

Editing and research by **Candace E. West**
Maps by **Norma Andriani Eka Putri**

ISBN-13: 978-1-943169-20-7

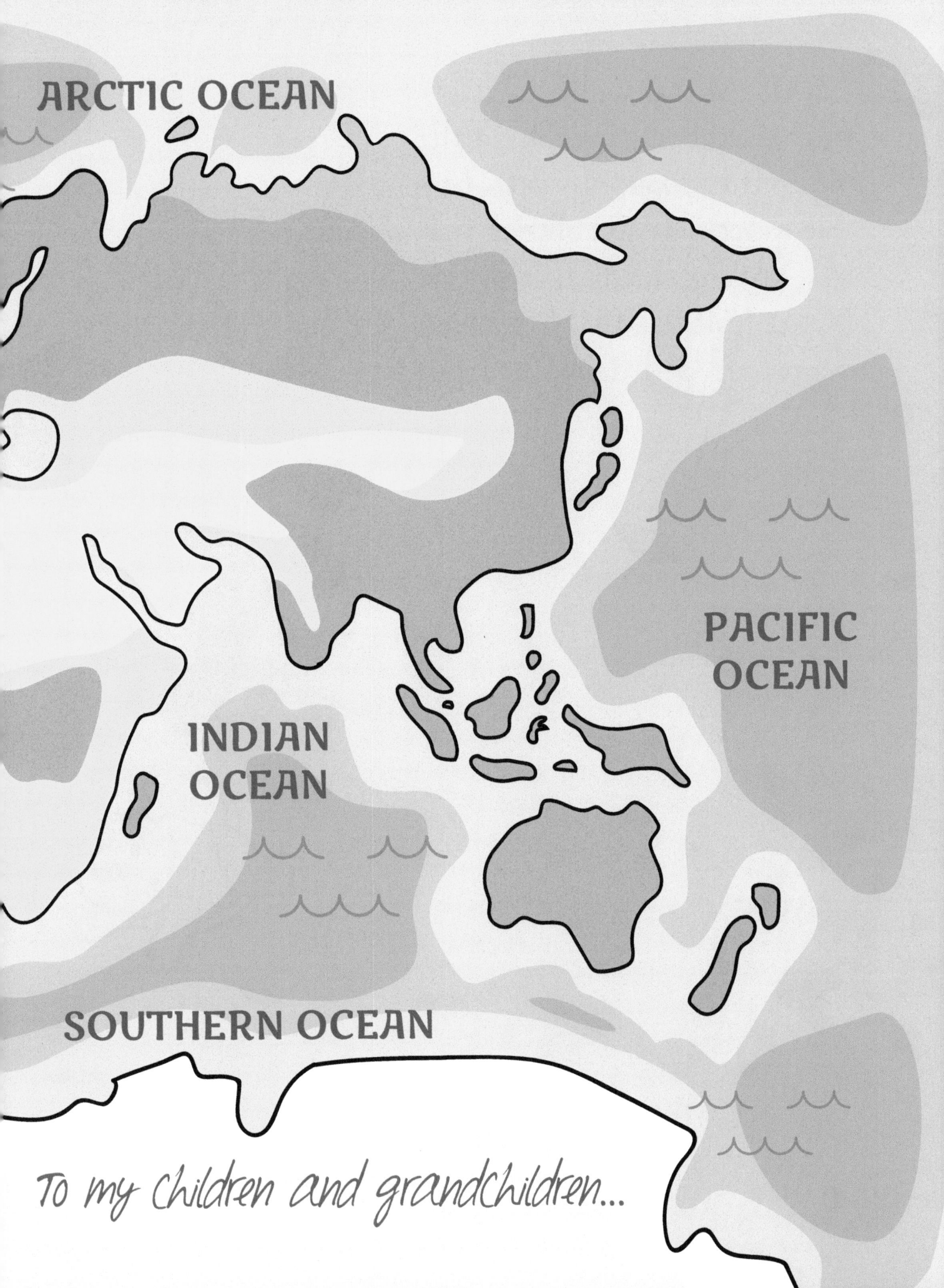

ARCTIC OCEAN

PACIFIC OCEAN

INDIAN OCEAN

SOUTHERN OCEAN

To my children and grandchildren...

Swift Walker walked faster than everybody. Even his little dog couldn't keep up with him. He never rode his bike or the bus, and he didn't like to ride in the family van. He walked everywhere and he walked fast.

His sister would say, "One day you'll walk so fast, you won't be able to stop!"

One cool fall day, just after lunch, Swift took a walk. A fast walk, of course. As Swift walked, he could hear the leaves crunch. He loved the sound of the leaves going crunch, crunch, crunch under his feet. All of a sudden,

Swift looked down because his feet were walking all on their own. His sister was right. They would not stop! Before he knew it, Swift had walked so far, all he could see was water, water everywhere!

Where is Swift Walker now?

THE ARCTIC OCEAN!

Large chunks of ice covered the ocean.
Right before his very eyes were two white polar bears
looking for yummy fish.

Are they hungry?
Watch out Swift!

GREENLAND

CANADA

He kept right on walking along The Arctic Ocean, through
Canada, Greenland, Norway, and Russia,
all the way to Japan.

Where is Swift Walker now?

NORWAY

RUSSIA

THE PACIFIC OCEAN.

Now this ocean was enormous. The Pacific Ocean made the Arctic Ocean seem tiny.

Just then, Swift spotted a sea lion playing in the water.

Water splashed him right on the nose.

Watch out Swift!

He kept right on walking along
The Pacific Ocean, through Japan,
Taiwan, and Vietnam, all the way
past Cambodia.

Where is Swift Walker now?

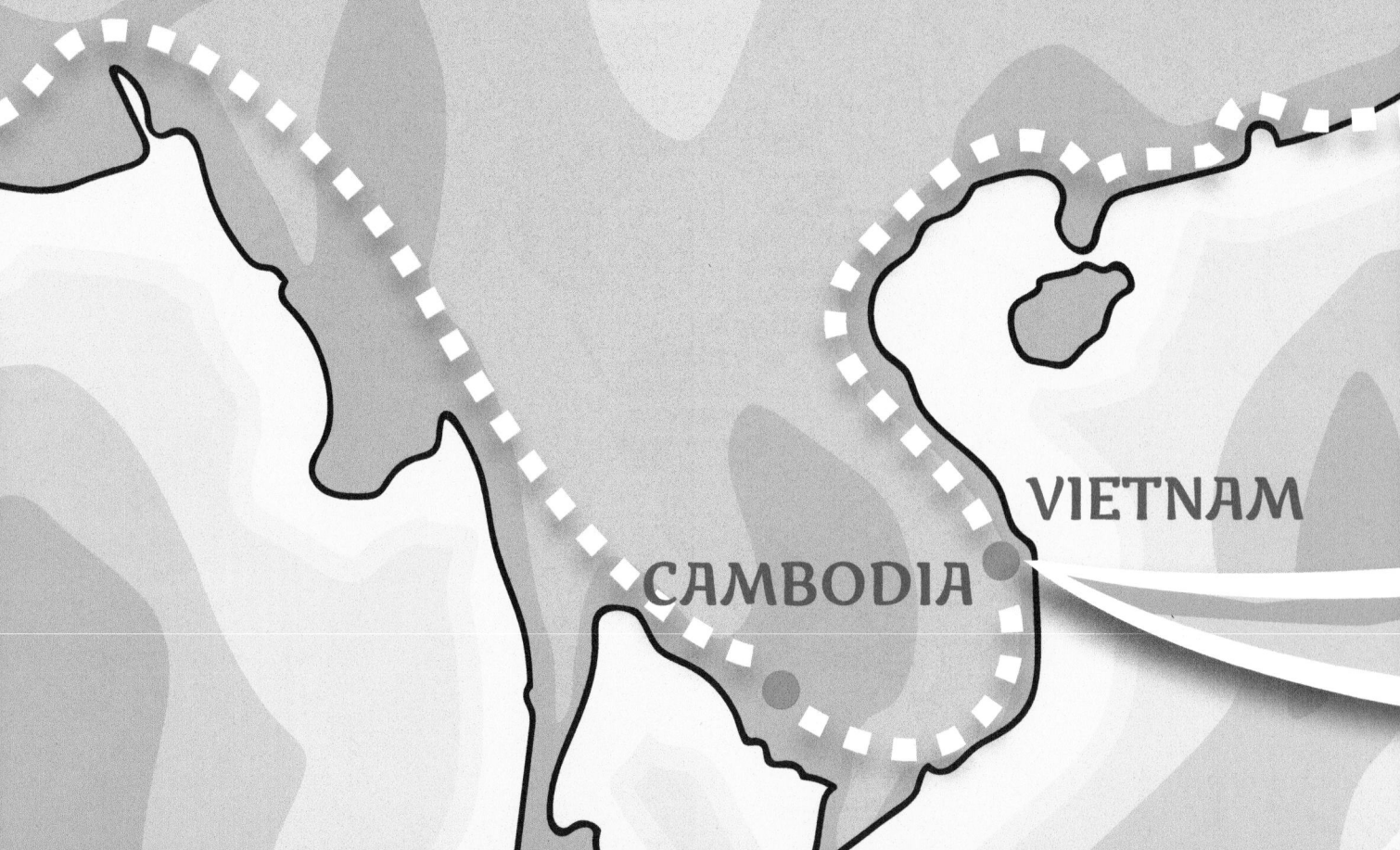

CAMBODIA

VIETNAM

JAPAN

TAIWAN

THE INDIAN OCEAN.

This ocean was smaller than the Pacific Ocean but bigger than the Arctic.

To his surprise, he spotted baby sea turtles racing towards the shore. They were so small and cute.

Watch out Swift!

Please don't step on them!

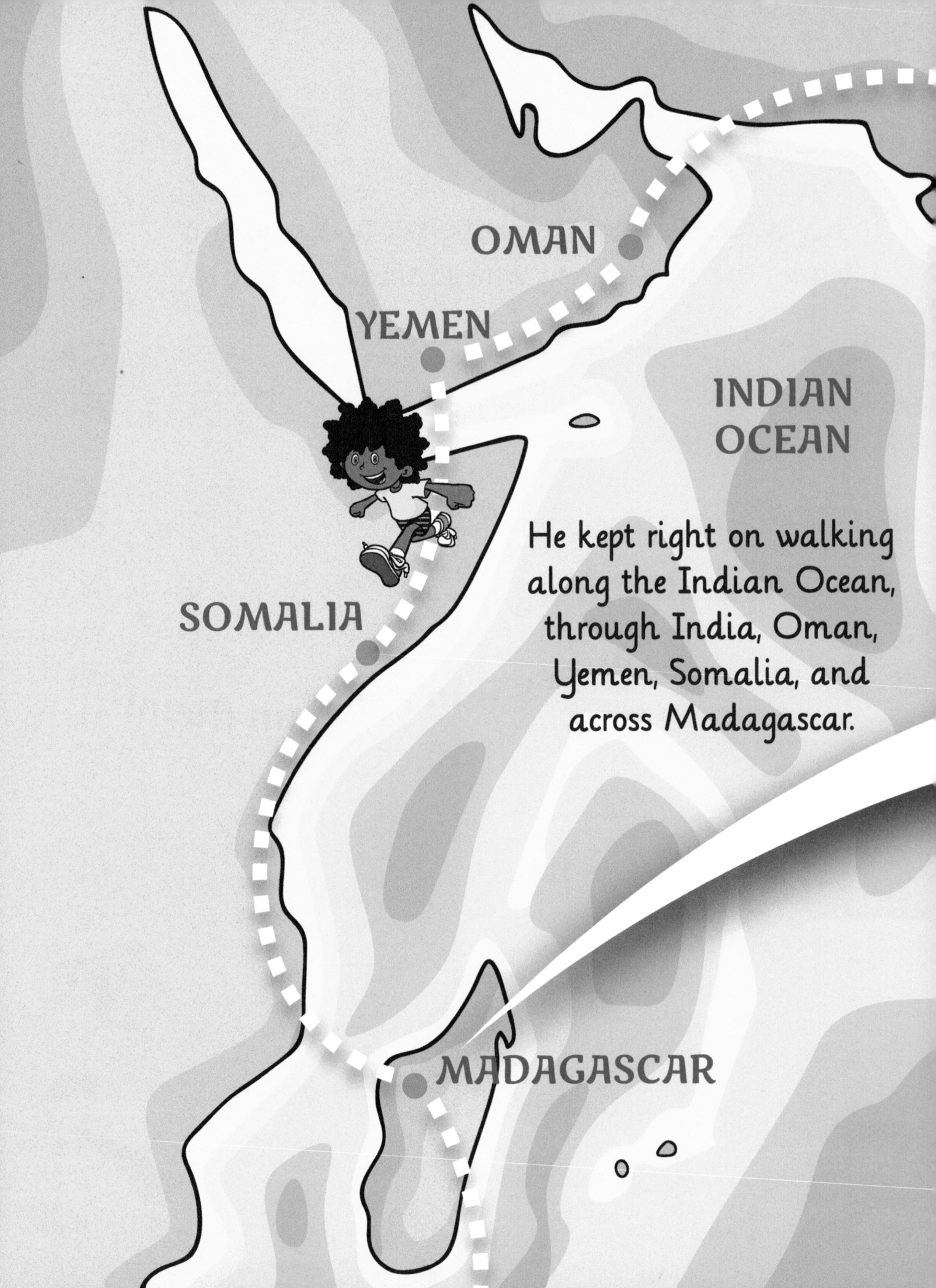

OMAN

YEMEN

INDIAN
OCEAN

SOMALIA

He kept right on walking
along the Indian Ocean,
through India, Oman,
Yemen, Somalia, and
across Madagascar.

MADAGASCAR

INDIA

Where is Swift Walker now?

THE SOUTHERN OCEAN,
also known as the Antarctic ocean

It looked like the ocean wrapped around all of Antarctica. Waddling along were colonies of tall, pudgy penguins.

Watch out Swift!

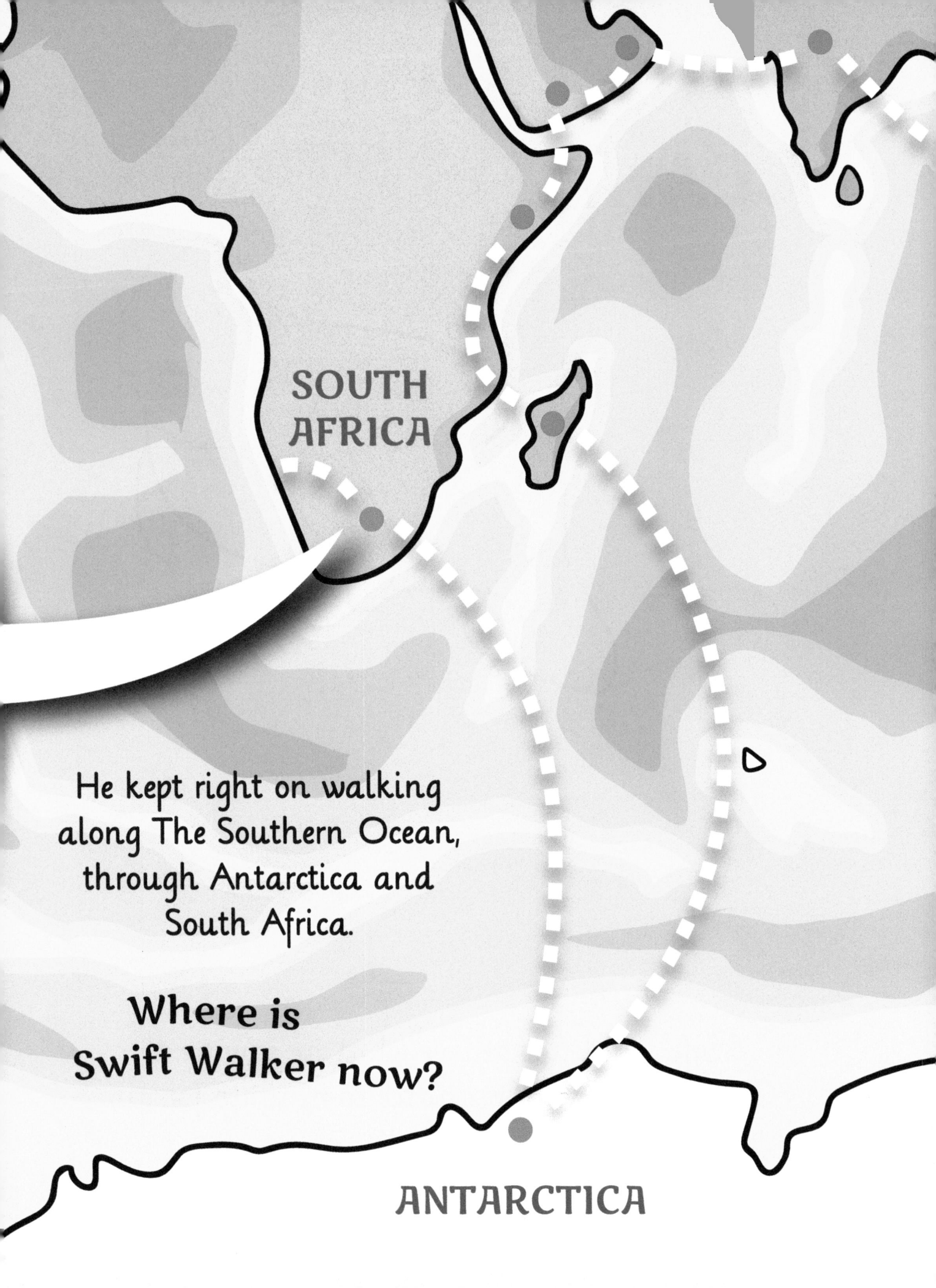

SOUTH
AFRICA

He kept right on walking along The Southern Ocean, through Antarctica and South Africa.

Where is Swift Walker now?

ANTARCTICA

THE ATLANTIC OCEAN.

Swift could not believe what he saw next!
Could it be? A big manatee coming up for air.

"Did the manatee see me?" Swift thought.

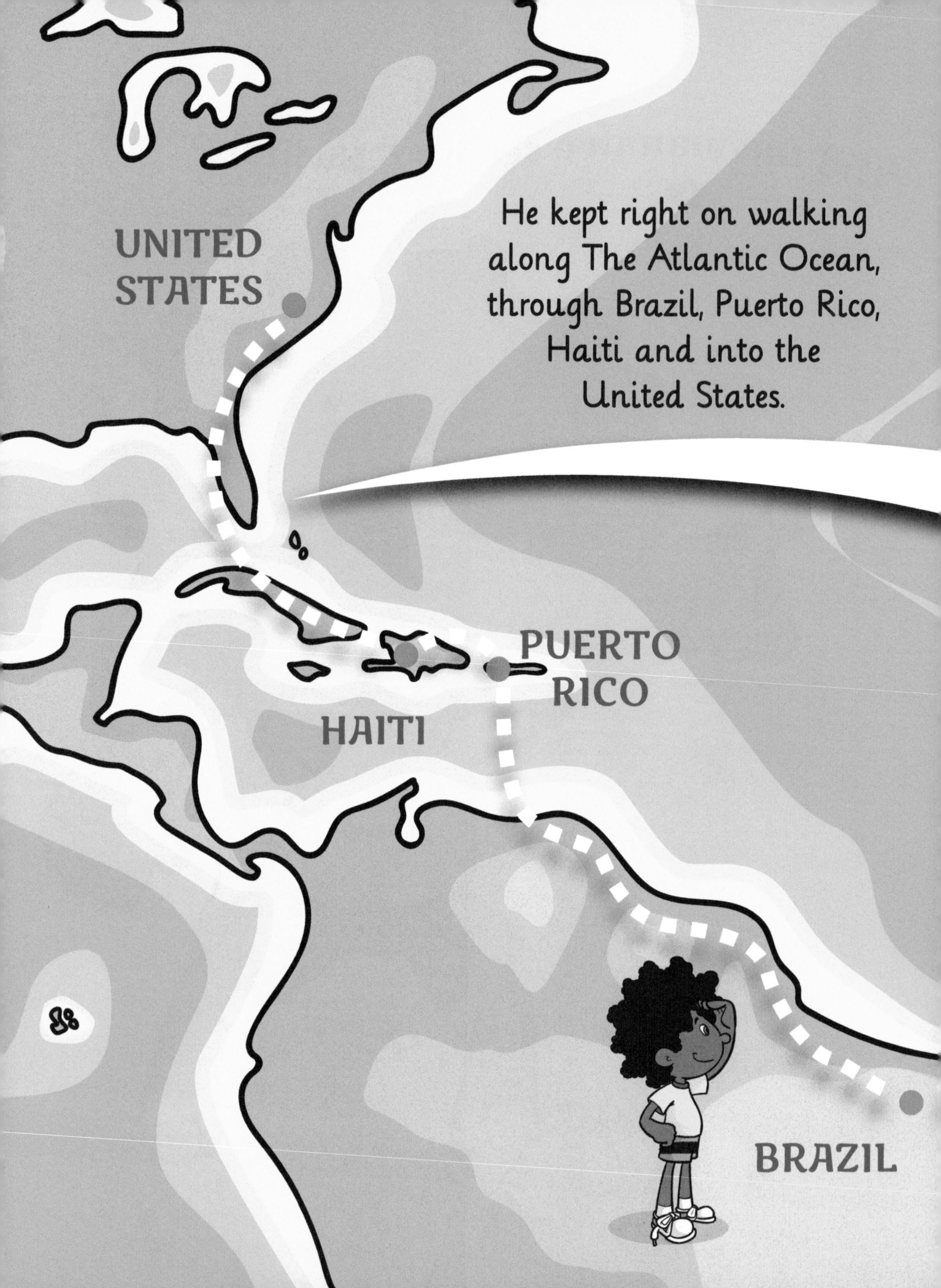

He kept right on walking along The Atlantic Ocean, through Brazil, Puerto Rico, Haiti and into the United States.

Where is Swift Walker now?

In his front yard. No water in sight. Just then, Swift saw his dad. His dad said,

"Son, you're just in time for dinner!"

Swift was too excited to think about dinner, so he began to tell his dad about his great adventure.

"I saw all five oceans today!"
His dad looked very surprised and smiled.
"Son, I think you might have super powers!"

Super powers!

"Wow!" he said. "Amazing!"

OCEANS

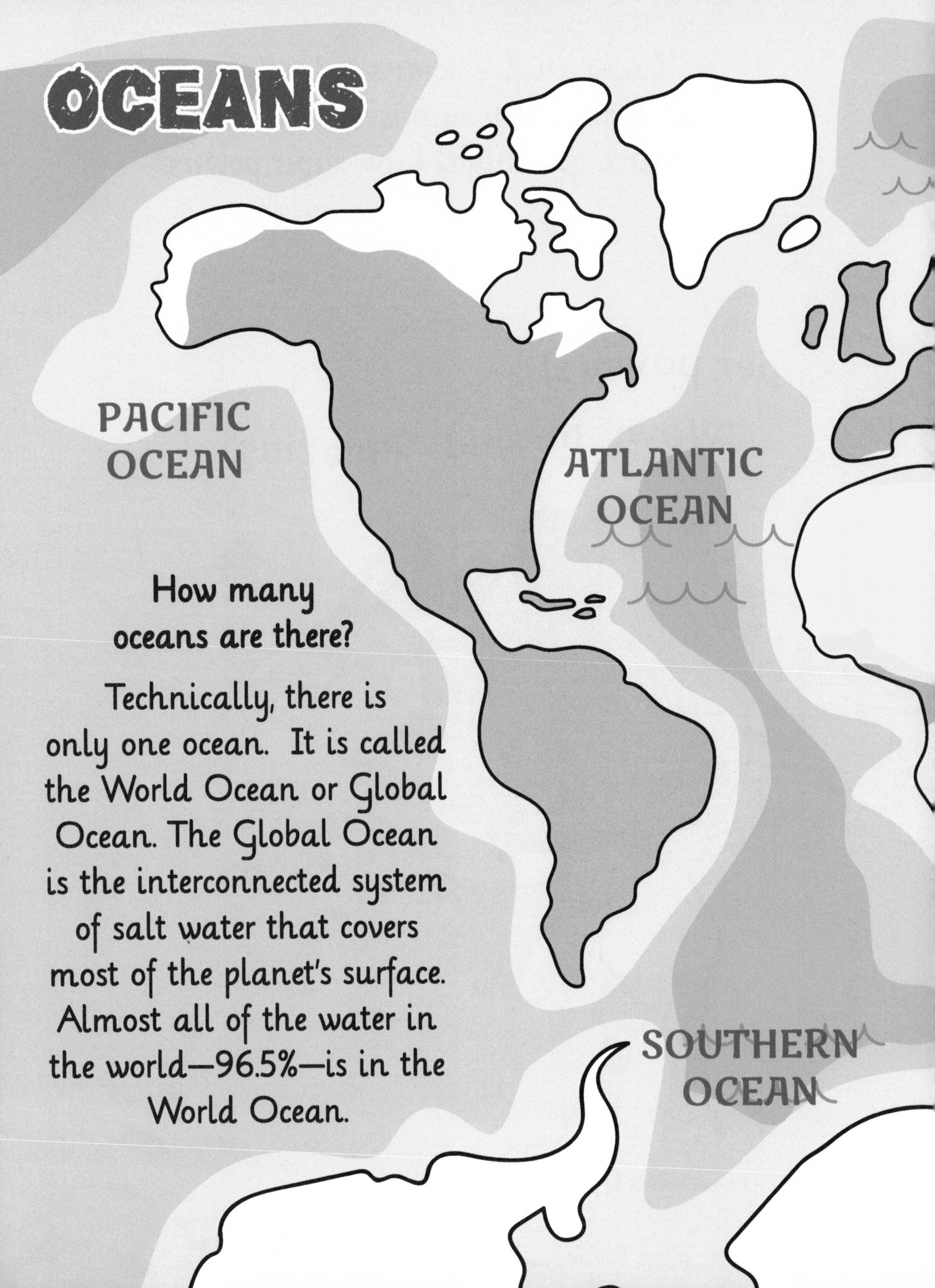

PACIFIC
OCEAN

ATLANTIC
OCEAN

SOUTHERN
OCEAN

How many oceans are there?

Technically, there is only one ocean. It is called the World Ocean or Global Ocean. The Global Ocean is the interconnected system of salt water that covers most of the planet's surface. Almost all of the water in the world—96.5%—is in the World Ocean.

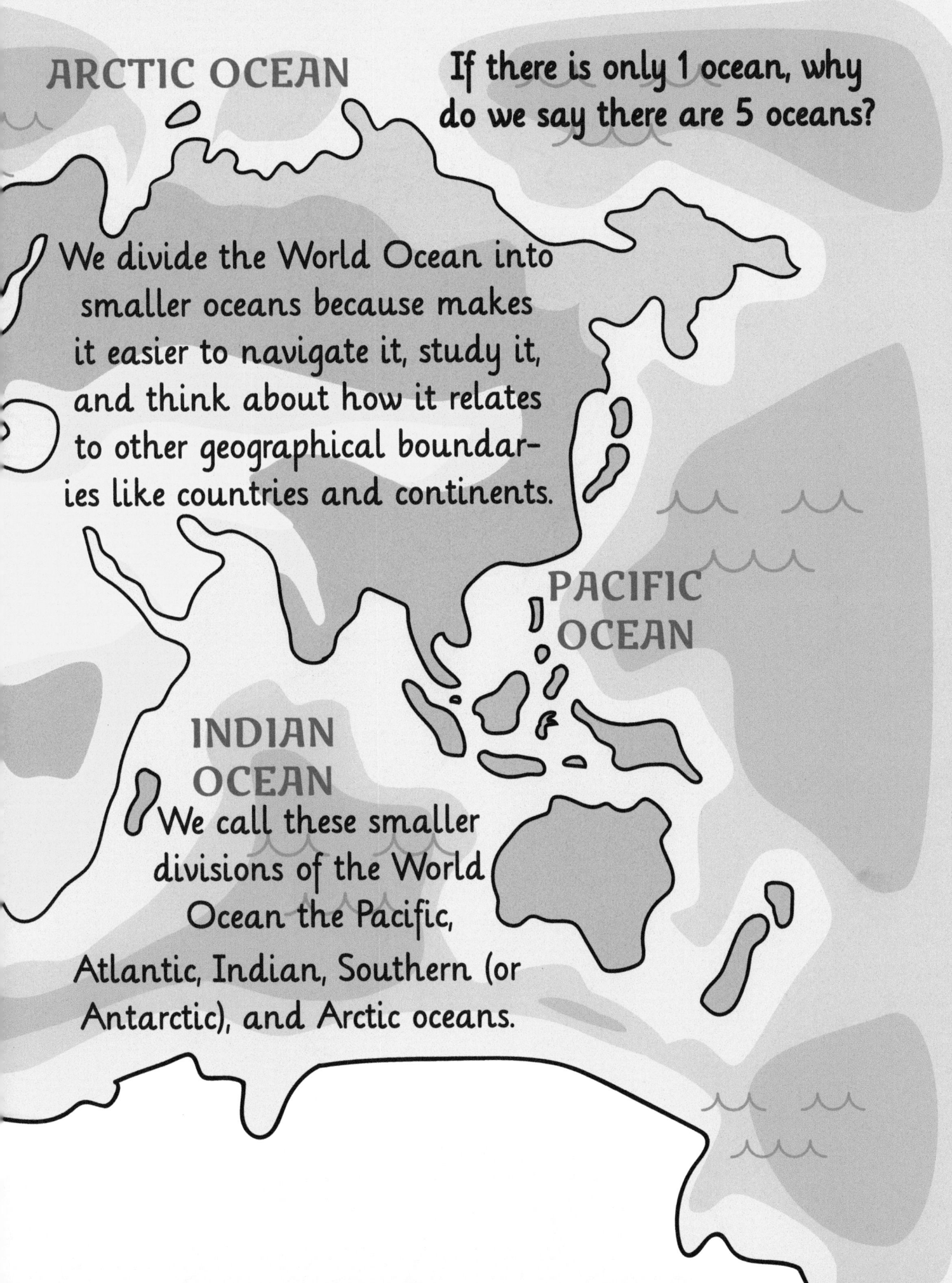

ARCTIC OCEAN

If there is only 1 ocean, why do we say there are 5 oceans?

We divide the World Ocean into smaller oceans because makes it easier to navigate it, study it, and think about how it relates to other geographical boundaries like countries and continents.

PACIFIC OCEAN

INDIAN OCEAN

We call these smaller divisions of the World Ocean the Pacific, Atlantic, Indian, Southern (or Antarctic), and Arctic oceans.

THE ARCTIC OCEAN!

The smallest, shallowest, and coldest ocean is the Arctic Ocean.

THE PACIFIC OCEAN.

The largest ocean is the Pacific. It is also the deepest ocean. The deepest part of the Pacific, known as the Challenger Deep, is about 36,200 feet. That's almost 7 miles!

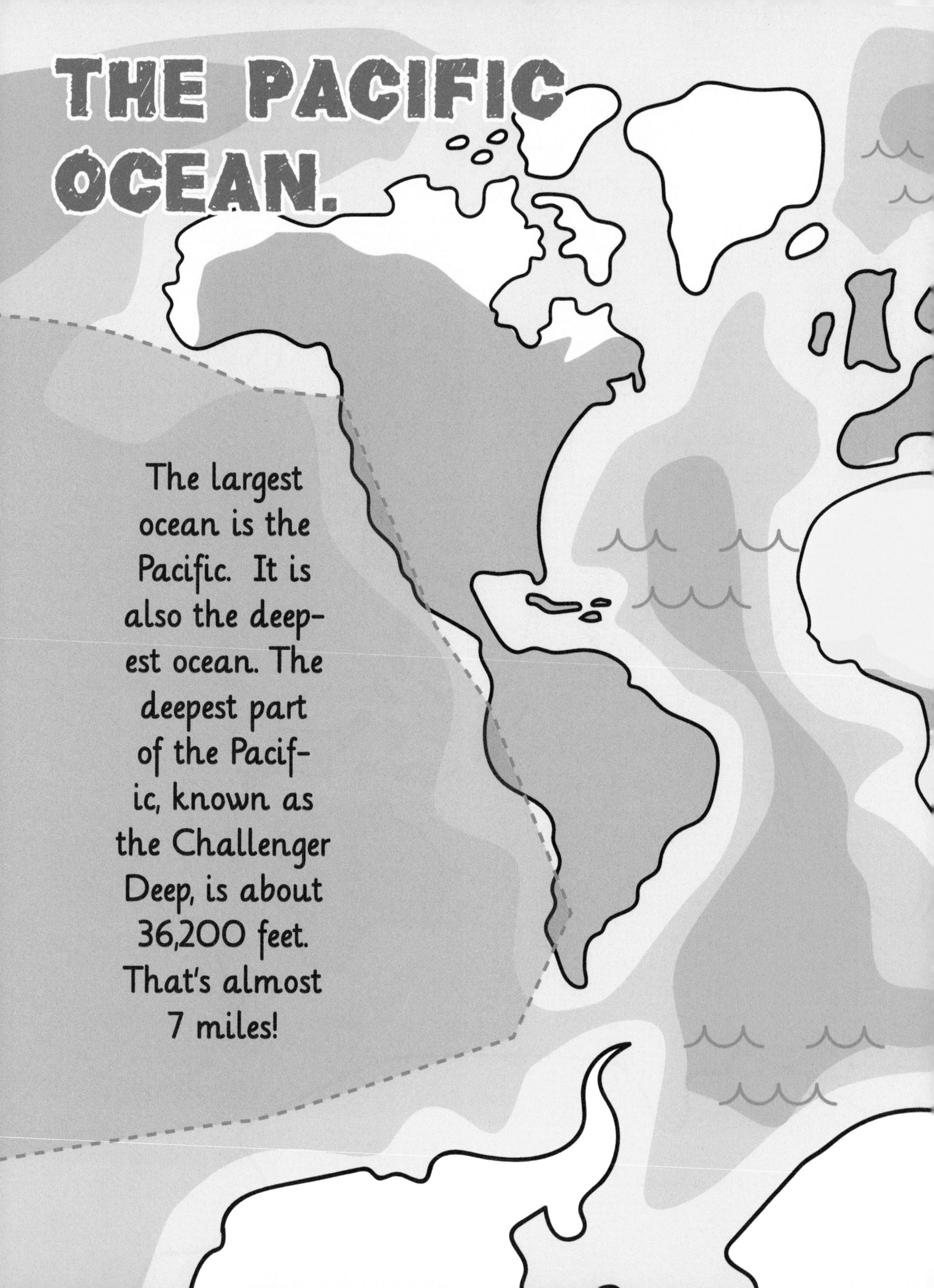

THE INDIAN OCEAN.

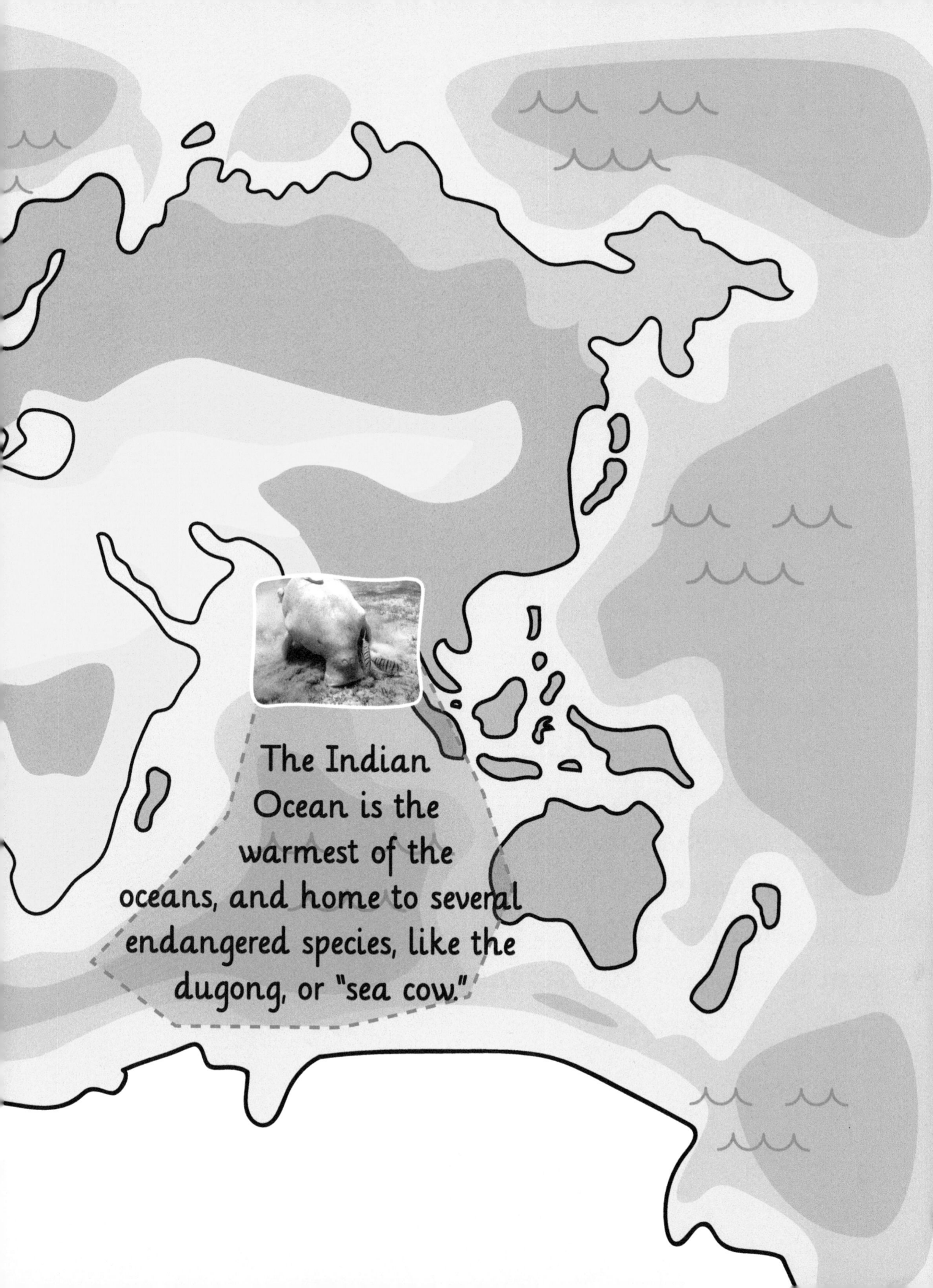

The Indian Ocean is the warmest of the oceans, and home to several endangered species, like the dugong, or "sea cow."

THE SOUTHERN OCEAN,

The Southern or Antarctic Ocean is mostly surrounded by other oceans instead of land. Mapmakers, governments, and oceanographers do not all agree on where the borders of the Southern Ocean are, or even if it counts as a separate ocean.

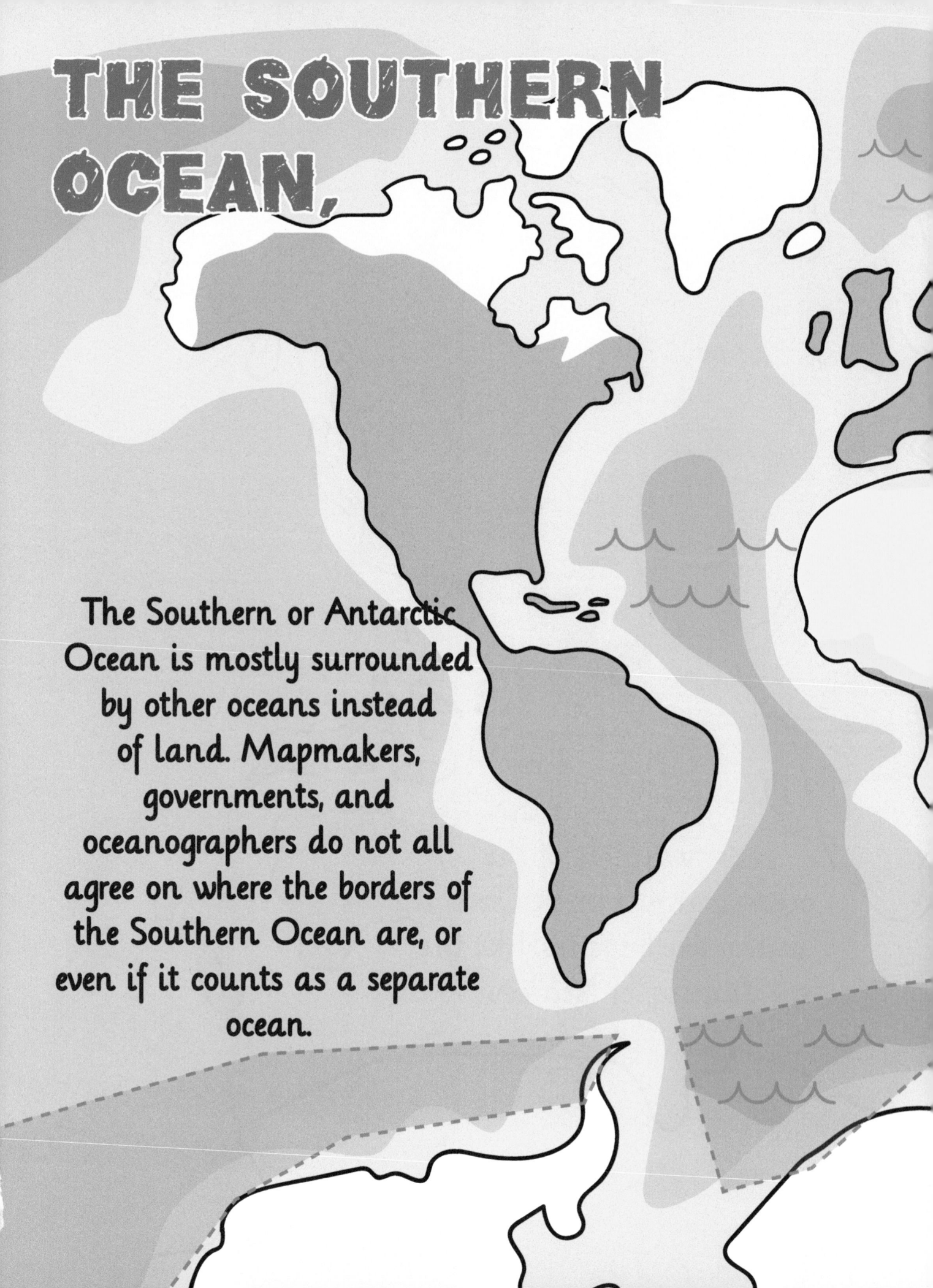

THE ATLANTIC OCEAN.

The Atlantic Ocean is the saltiest ocean despite having some of the Earth's largest rivers draining into it. The Amazon River in South America, the Mississippi River in North America, and The Congo River in Africa all drain into the Atlantic Ocean.

TRAVEL THE WORLD

ARCTIC

GREENLAND

CANADA

NORTH AMERICA

POTOMAC RIVER

AUKE BAY

ATLANTIC OCEAN

PACIFIC OCEAN

HORSEHOE BEND

UNITED STATES

SAHARA DESSERT

HAITI

PUERTO RICO

MOUNT COTOPAXI

AMAZON RAINFOREST

SOUTH AMERICA

BRAZIL

ATACAMA DESERT

ATLANTIC OCEAN

OCEANS JOURNEY
CONTINENTAL JOURNEY

WITH SWIFT WALKER

OCEAN
NORTH CAPE
NORWAY
ST. BASIL'S CATHEDRAL
RUSSIA
SIBERIA
EUROPE
EIFFEL TOWER
ASIA
YANGTZE RIVER
JAPAN
NILE RIVER
INDIA
TAIWAN
OMAN
TAJ MAHAL
VIETNAM
YEMEN
AFRICA
CAMBODIA
PACIFIC OCEAN
SERENGETI
SOMALIA
INDIAN OCEAN
Mt. KILIMANJARO
SOUTH AFRICA
MADAGASCAR
AUSTRALIA
KANAGRA FALLS
HARBOUR BRIDGE
SOUTHERN OCEAN
ANTARCTICA
OBSERVATION HILL

About the Author

Verlyn Tarlton, a native Washingtonian, is a mother, wife, speaker, and author. She got her love of reading and writing from her late grandfather, Ethelbert W. Haskins, who was a university professor in Washington, DC. She has always been passionate about reading, writing, and teaching. She especially wants to pass on her love of reading and adventure to young children and encourage them to dream BIG!

www.facebook.com/VerlynTarlton

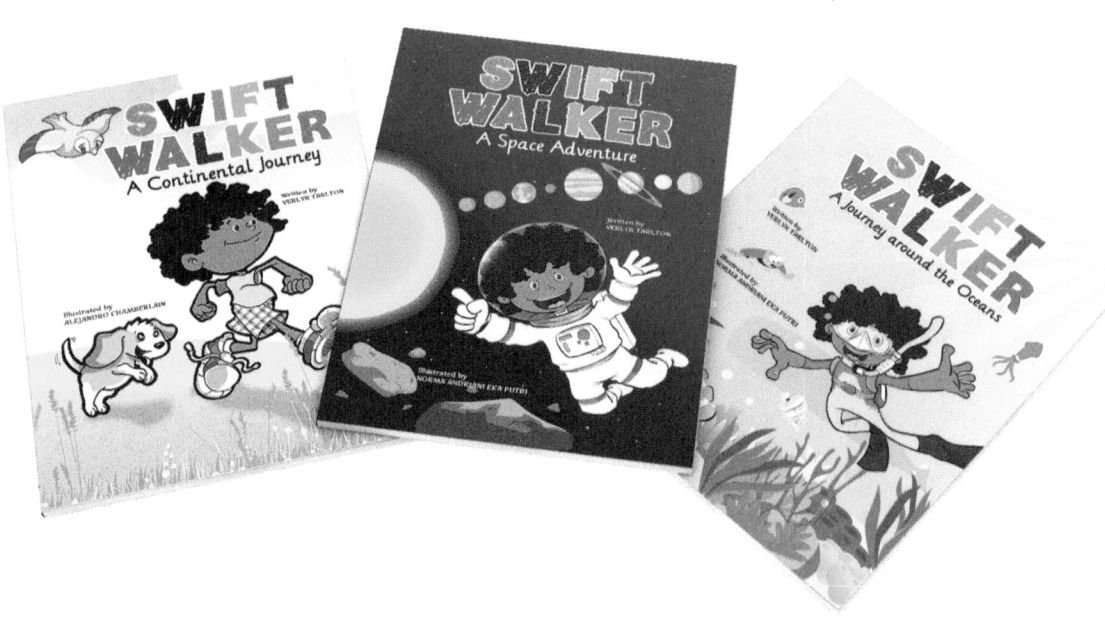